I HAVE THE WATCH

BECOMING A LEADER WORTH FOLLOWING

JON S. RENNIE

FOREWORD BY JOHN BRUBAKER, AUTHOR OF *SEEDS OF SUCCESS*

I Have the Watch: Becoming a Leader Worth Following
Jon S. Rennie

© 2019 by Jon S. Rennie

Requests for permission should be made in writing to:

Jon S. Rennie
Deck & Conn, LLC
437 Kings Glen Way
Wake Forest, NC 27587
www.jonsrennie.com
email: jon@jonsrennie.com

Edited by: Mary Lou Reynolds
Cover and interior design: Daniel Yeager, Nu-Image Design

Printed in the United States of America

Library of Congress Cataloging In Publication Data is available from the author upon request.

ISBN 978-1099487095

CONTENTS

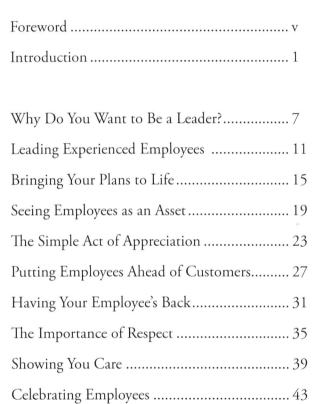

FOREWORD

Most forewords tell you about the book you're about to read, but this isn't most forewords and this sure isn't like most books. So instead of telling you about the book you're going to read, I'd rather share a personal story with you that illustrates precisely why you should zero in on what Jon Rennie has to say in this book.

My dad used the expression "Got Your Six" all the time. He was a fighter pilot in World War II and when I was little, I asked him what it meant. He explained it's a military term that fighter pilots use with one another to reference their plane's rear, the six o'clock position. In other words, it's your most vulnerable position because you can't see what's behind you. It's why pilots have wingmen and travel together. If your wingman says, "I've got your six," it means "I've got your back."

The expression also speaks well to the loyalty and co-operation you find on any type of successful team. Great leaders like Jon Rennie have their team members' six.

It's also the most powerful leadership lesson I learned my senior year in college as a varsity lacrosse player at Fairleigh Dickinson University. After a series of injuries as a junior, I was finally healthy and was expected to be one of the best players and leaders on my team. Before I came back for my senior year, I set goals over the summer that I would be one of the leading scorers and a team captain.

One particular preseason practice is permanently etched in my memory. It was early morning on a Saturday. Practice always ended with the team collectively having to finish the dreaded sprint-ladders under a prescribed amount of time. If everyone made the cutoff time, conditioning was over. If someone didn't, EVERYONE ran it again until they did. (If you don't know what a sprint-ladder is, it's a series of ten timed sprints starting at 20 yards that get 20 yards longer each time, up to 200 yards.)

As you can imagine, it's easier in the beginning and gets progressively harder, especially if you're out of shape, and it's really tough if you're overweight to boot. One of our walk-on players, Jason, fit both descriptions.

A sophomore defenseman, Bill Hickey, and I were pushing each other in sprints at the end of practice. About halfway through the ladder, several of us knew, based on our experience, that we were going to finish ahead of the 42-second 200-yard cutoff. So as we were "lapping" some other players, we'd yell at them to hurry up and run faster. When Bill didn't pipe up and join us, I immediately began judging him and wasn't impressed.

Then, an interesting thing happened. After almost everyone on the team finished the sprint ladder, Jason was still plodding away down the field. Everyone was shouting at him (some positive, some negative) – everyone except for one person. While the other teammates were running their mouths, Bill went back for Jason and ran with him. He talked to him, made him laugh, and encouraged him as they finished together. Simply put, Bill had his back while everyone else was talking about him behind his back… myself included.

I learned a lot about what leadership REALLY was that day. Much like you're about to learn what leadership really is as you read Jon's book. Lessons like:

- Leadership by example isn't everything. People need you to verbalize it and do so in a positive way. Leadership is coaching, and a lot of times coaching is actually coaxing. What I mean is that it isn't just about strategy or simply setting the right example. It's also about providing encouragement and positive reinforcement.

- Leadership isn't about pushing people; it's about pulling people. You can't push a rope.

- People don't follow titles. They follow courage.

- When you have someone's six, you may be located behind that person, but you're still leading. You can lead by making sure others feel safe because they trust you won't let anything blindside them from behind.

- You need your best players to also be your hardest workers. As a leader, your work isn't done when "your work" is done. It's also your job to help others succeed.

When I wasn't named one of the team captains that year, I knew exactly why. The long, hard lesson I learned was that it's more important to be the best player FOR the team than the best player ON the team. Quite frankly, I was neither. Bill Hickey was definitely the best player for our team.

Fast-forward 24 years: Bill Hickey is now Sgt. William Hickey of the Lancaster, Pennsylvania, police force.

I share this with you because he and Jon Rennie remind me a lot of one another. I'm honored to know them because they are both selfless leaders who put their people first and proudly serve their communities.

If you're reading this, you're a member of Jon Rennie's community and I want you to know he's definitely "got your six." Jon walks his talk and is a man of high moral character in an industry rife with charlatans. The world needs more Jon Rennies because we are in an era where many leaders are more worried about covering their own six than having someone else's back.

As Jon so aptly says, leadership is indeed a people business. Which begs the important question: Who's got your six in your organization? And more importantly, whose six do you have?

That's the test of whether or not you're a leader worth following.

If you want to elevate and separate yourself from the competition, you've got the right book in your hands. Through his experience as an officer in the U.S. Navy and the CEO of a highly successful company, Jon delivers a series of very compelling, powerful lessons in this book.

I promise this book will do two things for you: It will challenge you and it will change you. It will *challenge* you to take a long, hard look at the way you lead and see things through a different lens. And that's precisely the point: In order to achieve a level of success you haven't had before, you have to be willing to lead at a higher level than you ever have before. And, if you apply Jon's timeless wisdom, it will *change* you. You will transform into a heart-centered leader who walks your talk and puts the organization's most valuable resource first… its people.

So grab a highlighter, a pen, and plenty of paper to take notes. You're about to learn some incredibly valuable strategies to tangibly show your teammates and customers you've got their six. And in the process, you'll see that Jon has yours.

Be Your Best,
John Brubaker
CoachBru.com

INTRODUCTION

Leadership is all about people. It is not about organizations. It is not about plans. It is not about strategies. It is all about people – motivating people to get the job done. You have to be people-centered.

– Colin Powell

Almost 30 years ago in December of 1990, I walked into the engine room of the nuclear submarine *USS Tennessee*. With a little apprehension, I entered an area called Instrument Alley and met my team for the first time. Instrument Alley is the nickname for a set of two long electrical panels that sit behind the reactor compartment, and they contain all the reactor instruments. My job was to lead the small team who maintained and operated these complex reactor systems. I was their leader. I had the watch.

This was my first leadership job. I went on to serve five years as a Naval Officer and led dozens of sailors in the high-paced, complex, and often dangerous world of underwater warfare before leaving for the corporate world. In business, I worked in several department management positions at ABB, a multinational engineering company, before being promoted to my first manufacturing oper-

1

ation. At just 32 years old, I moved my family to South Carolina to became plant manager of a small manufacturing operation with 160 employees, and I've been leading industrial businesses ever since.

In my career, I have led nine manufacturing businesses for four companies, including *Peak Demand,* the company I co-founded and currently serve as CEO. I have had the fortune to lead some amazing teams of up to 600 people and businesses with $250M in sales. The single most important lesson I've learned during these years is that *leadership matters*. Leadership can make a significant difference in the performance of any organization.

If you're reading this book, you understand the importance of leadership and, if you've been a leader for any length of time, you've probably discovered that leadership is a paradox. It is both simple and complex at the same time. Like chess, it takes a short time to learn but a lifetime to master. This is why there are more than 15,000 books written on the subject of leadership. Each one has added to the collective understanding of this simple but complex subject. My hope is that this book adds to your understanding of leadership and motivates you to become a better leader.

No book about leadership would be complete without a definition of leadership. In this case, I prefer to use one that was written by *New York Times* bestseller author and business leader, Kevin Kruse. He says, "Leadership is a process of social influence, which maximizes the efforts of [people], towards the achievement of a goal." This is my preferred definition. In it, he describes the three most important elements of leadership – people, influence, and a goal.

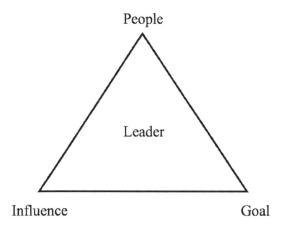

The Leadership Triangle

The best way to visualize this definition is with a triangle where people are placed on the top point and influence and goal are on the two bottom points. I call this the leadership triangle. I put people on top as a simple reminder that, in leadership, people should be the top priority. I then place the leader in the center of the triangle. The leader is the conductor with the job of coordinating and balancing these three elements. A leader must define the goal, build up the team, and motivate them properly to reach that goal. If a leader fails to focus on any of these three critical elements, they will fail. If they try to put themselves on the top of the triangle, they will fail as well.

This book is a curated collection of articles I have written over the past five years. On my website, *jonsrennie. com*, I write about various topics like leadership, business, entrepreneurship, and the military, but the articles selected for this book all deal with leadership. Specifically, each one deals with the important element of leading people. I share my experiences in nearly 30 years of leading people in both the military and business. As you read through each chapter, think about the leadership triangle. Use that as your reference point. Look for how the leader in each story balances the elements of people, influence, and goals. You will find times when leaders have placed themselves on top of the triangle or when they are not even on the triangle. Look for stories when the goal has been moved to the top or when influence is too small. If you think about the leadership triangle, you will gain a deeper understanding of each chapter.

Finally, I should explain my motivation for writing this book. I'm concerned about the state of leadership. By all accounts, there is a leadership crisis in business today. Even though our collective understanding of leadership has never been stronger, our practice of leadership remains subpar at best. According to *Gallup*, 70% of employees are disengaged at work and half of U.S. employees are actively searching for a new job. The statistics confirm there is a leadership problem in America. If that isn't enough to convince you, just think of the conversations you are having at work about terrible bosses and the consequences of bad leadership. I hear at least one story a day about a bad boss, and I'm sure you do as well. You might even be working for a bad boss right now.

My goal for this book is straightforward – to provide practical leadership advice that you will use. The book is not written from a theoretical perspective. This is real-world advice written from a hands-on perspective. It is provided with the intent that you'll find nuggets of wisdom that you will actually use in your role as a leader. My hope is that one day we can all eliminate bad bosses and put people back on top of the leadership triangle. When it comes right down to it, leadership is a people business. If you ever forget that, you will never be a great leader.

WHY DO YOU WANT TO BE A LEADER?

Great leaders don't set out to be a leader...
they set out to make a difference.
– Lisa Haisha

There is a crisis in America. There is a shortage of good leaders, and it seems to be getting worse. The problem is people are choosing leadership for the wrong reasons.

Susan Cain, author of *Quiet: The Power of Introverts in a World That Can't Stop Talking*, is changing how people think about introverts. While she is widely known for her writings on this subject, it's her thoughts on leadership that got my attention. In a *New York Times* article called "Not Leadership Material? Good. The World Needs Followers," she explains that in America today we have "glorified" leadership. So much so that people are taking on leadership roles for the wrong reasons. They are choosing to become leaders to get recognition, more money, or to help advance their careers. She explains:

> Perhaps the biggest disservice done by the
> outsize glorification of "leadership skills" is
> the practice of leadership itself – it hollows

7

it out, it empties it of meaning. It attracts those who are motivated by the spotlight rather than by the ideas and people they serve. It teaches [people] to be a leader for the sake of being in charge, rather than in the name of a cause or idea they care about deeply. The difference between the two states of mind is profound.

While the focus of her article is to point out the importance of those who don't choose a leadership path, she indirectly uncovers the crisis in the current state of leadership. There is a shortage of good leaders. People are choosing to lead for the wrong reasons, which is why there are so many poor leaders.

If you want to be a leader, the first question you should ask yourself is *why?* Why do you want to be a leader? If you are choosing this role for the paycheck, the title, the prestige, the power, or the trappings of the position, you are going to be sadly disappointed. Leadership is difficult. Being responsible for motivating a group of people to accomplish a goal isn't something you choose to do without careful consideration.

Let me suggest three questions to ask yourself:

Do you have a passion for leadership? Just like selecting any career, ask yourself if you have the passion to lead. To be a leader means you have the full responsibility of an organization and all the people associated with it. It means you will be accountable for everything that happens on your watch. It is a difficult and sometimes lonely job that demands a 24/7 commitment. Ask yourself if you have the passion and desire to be a great leader.

Do you care deeply about the idea or organization? As the leader, all eyes will be on you. Your attitudes toward the mission will reverberate throughout the organization. As a conductor, your team will be taking cues from you. If you care deeply about the organization's mission, they will as well. If you are half-hearted, they will be too. Ask yourself if you care deeply about the idea or organization you will lead.

Do you love people? The one thing I see most in poor leaders is their negative attitude towards people. Leadership is a people business. Your entire job is to motivate people towards accomplishing a goal. Unfortunately, many people who don't like people choose leadership. I understand. People are messy. They have issues, problems, emotions, relationships, and baggage. But your job is to see past the flaws, love your people, and motivate them to do great things. You can't be a great leader if you don't love people.

As Susan Cain points out, people are choosing to lead for the wrong reasons. The result is a hollowed-out, empty version of leadership that's not good for people or organizations. Leadership, like any other profession, requires a specific set of skills. If you don't have them, you shouldn't pursue a leadership path.

Ask yourself these questions and determine if you have a passion to lead. Find out if you care deeply about the mission. Understand your view of people and what it takes to lead them. If you choose to lead, be a great leader. Honestly, we need better, not more, leaders.

LEADING EXPERIENCED EMPLOYEES

If you once forfeit the confidence of your fellow citizens, you can never regain their respect and esteem.
– Abraham Lincoln

At 32 years old, I was promoted to plant manager, although I had never run a manufacturing plant in my life. After I left the Navy, I spent five years working for ABB, a global engineering company, as a design engineer, a quality manager, and an engineering manager. I had never worked in manufacturing or production, yet my boss at the time felt that I had the leadership skills to take on the responsibility of leading a manufacturing plant in our division.

Upon arriving at this manufacturing operation, I soon realized there was a lot to do. There were quality problems that needed to be fixed, cost challenges that needed to be addressed, and morale issues to be confronted. I was concerned I might be in over my head. I was the youngest manager this plant had ever had and I didn't want to fail.

What made it more intimidating was that the managers and workforce at this facility were all older and more experienced than I was. They knew far more than I did about how to run the plant. My challenge was to figure out how to lead this operation effectively while not knowing as much as my team.

Many leaders find themselves in situations like this. They're surrounded by people who are older and more experienced after a promotion or job change. It's easy to become intimidated. Leading employees who are older and more experienced can be a challenge. Many leaders make the mistake of trying to appear knowledgeable, to fake it, but it doesn't work on experienced employees.

The truth is that inexperienced leaders don't need to have all the answers to be successful but they need to be excellent at working with their teams. Fortunately, my past had prepared me well for leading in a situation like this. Even though I didn't have extensive manufacturing knowledge, I had previously led people who were older and more experienced than I was during my time in the Navy.

As a young junior officer fresh out of submarine school, I was assigned the reactor controls department on the *USS Tennessee*, where I led a team of veteran sailors who were talented and experienced. Despite my inexperience, I became an effective leader by learning, observing, listening, and engaging with my team. I took a humble approach and treated the skilled sailors with the respect they deserved. That prior experience prepared me well for my role as a 32-year-old plant manager.

Here are some of the things you can do to become an effective leader when you are young and inexperienced. They worked for me both in the Navy and at this manufacturing plant:

Listening. Probably the most important thing you need to do as a young or inexperienced leader is to listen to your team. Be curious. Listen to what's working and what's not. Ask good questions and engage your experienced employees in helping to find solutions.

Respect. It is extremely important to demonstrate respect for your new team. They will see you as an inexperienced leader so don't pretend you're an expert. It's alright to ask questions and defer to their expertise to help solve problems in areas where you lack proficiency.

Seek feedback. Talk to key leaders and employees and seek feedback. If you have a potential solution to a problem, run it by some of the experienced people and listen to their comments. Ask your employees if this has been tried before. Has it worked or failed? What did the previous managers get wrong? How can you do it differently? Engage and seek feedback from your team and you will avoid the pitfalls of going headlong into an activity that's destined to fail.

Experiment. Try incremental actions and look at the results. I like to start small and observe the response of the team. Do they get excited about this new initiative? Is this something you can build on? Who were the naysayers? Who were the cheerleaders? Experimenting can help you discover what's going to work and what isn't.

Learn. Continue to be curious and seek knowledge. Read about the issues affecting your industry. Understand the norms and standards. Study the products and services you're providing. Become knowledgeable in your new role. As your employees see you gain understanding, they'll increase their respect for you.

The bottom line is leading employees who are older and more experienced can be a challenge. You may be well outside your comfort zone, but that just means you need to be more engaged, active, and involved with your employees. Use these five actions to work with experienced employees to find the best way to improve the organization. Find out who your naysayers are, discover your cheerleaders, and uncover the opinion leaders in the group. Continue to grow and gain knowledge to earn respect. In the end, you'll find you can be very successful even though you don't have all the answers.

Bringing Your Plans to Life

A plan is only as good as those who see it through.
– Anonymous

"Officers and crew of the United States *Gerald R. Ford*, man our ship and bring her to life!" commanded Susan Ford Bales, daughter of President Ford and sponsor of the newest U.S. aircraft carrier, the USS *Gerald R. Ford*.

The command was answered by sailors in crisp, white uniforms peeling off formation and running to man the rails of the newest warship in the U.S. Navy. "Anchors Aweigh" played, horns blared, bells rang out, and the U.S. flag was raised to full mast. Within minutes, the captain was informed that "the ship is manned and ready and reports for duty to the fleet."

As I watched this emotional ceremony play out, I couldn't help but think about the powerful message that was being delivered. The imagery, the speeches, and the commands all communicated one point: The crew brings the ship to life.

As a business leader and former Naval Officer, I know this is true but it's easy to overlook. We get caught up in the importance of our business plans, strategic initiatives, and stretch goals. We forget that it's people who bring these plans to life. Without her crew, the $13 billion state-of-the-art nuclear-powered aircraft carrier is nothing but a hunk of cold steel sitting in the harbor. Without a dedicated team, our plans are dead as well.

How do we create a dedicated crew that will bring our plans to life?

Get people involved in the planning. When people are involved in creating the plans, they have more ownership. Annual off-site planning sessions are a great way to do this. If done right, these sessions can create energy, excitement, and bonding in the team. It also helps to focus the team on the key objectives for the year.

Communicate your plans in a straightforward manner. I've worked for three global companies and one of the things that frustrated me is how they communicated plans. Global companies are complex and their plans are complicated, but the communication process shouldn't be. Using 100+ PowerPoint slides to communicate your vision is not effective. Focus your plans into a handful of important points and use stories to illustrate your message. Doing this will get more people on board.

Seek feedback and be willing to adjust your plans. Rolling out new plans in small groups is an effective way to let teams absorb the message and provide feedback. Listening to feedback is critical for two main reasons: (1) It allows teams to internalize the plan and (2) it allows you to learn things you hadn't considered. Seeking feedback will help get even more people on board.

Corral the naysayers. Despite your best efforts, there will always be those on your team who don't buy into the message. It's important to identify those people and meet with them individually. If they have constructive feedback, hear them out. Everyone deals with change differently. If they are simply unwilling to get on board, it might be time to part ways. Naysayers can have a negative impact on morale and can hurt the overall team's performance. It's better to deal with the problems than to ignore them.

A ship is nothing without her crew and a plan is nothing without people to implement it. If you spend a long time developing a plan, spend twice that amount of effort getting people on board. Without a dedicated crew, your plan is going nowhere. Get more people involved in the planning process and work on a straightforward communications plan. Listen to feedback and adjust accordingly. Most importantly, corral the naysayers. If you do these things, you will build a crew to bring your plans to life.

Seeing Employees as an Asset

It's important to view employees for what they really are:
the core creators of value in your business.
— Leanne Armstrong

Companies often use the phrase "Our employees are our greatest asset," but their actions don't reflect this belief. In fact, more managers treat employees like an expense, something that needs to be eliminated. Consider this comment that a reader posted on my website: "Being an employee of several different companies, I can honestly say that I've felt like nothing more than a line item on a spreadsheet somewhere that an accountant is desperately trying to eliminate."

This is a common feeling for many employees and the problem may actually be related to accounting. Why? Because in accounting rules, employee costs are an expense.

Consider this: By accounting rules, the cost of workers, salaries, and benefits is treated as an expense on the income statement. In fact, personnel expense is one of the highest costs a company incurs. Many managers see this sizable cost every month and conclude people are expensive. They see people as a problem. By seeing people as a costly expenditure, these managers think that a quick way to more profits is by reducing people or salaries. They look at employees as a problem that must be reduced or eliminated.

Great leaders see things differently. They consider employees as an asset. In accounting terms, assets are company resources which have future economic value. Instead of seeing employees as a problem, these leaders see them as a valuable resource. They know people have the capability to grow sales, satisfy customers, improve processes, innovate products, and do countless other things that add value and grow both the top and bottom lines. In my years as a leader, I have seen countless examples of this.

The truth is, if you think of employees as an asset, you treat them differently. You understand the importance of keeping them happy and operating at peak performance. You recognize the importance of being a good leader. You realize your team will be at their best when they are loved, appreciated, respected, engaged, and acknowledged.

It seems simple to me but it's not practiced in most organizations. One of the problems is the lack of leadership training in business schools. Most graduate and undergraduate students take multiple courses in accounting but they may only attend one or two lectures on leadership. This results in sending young managers to the workplace with a belief that numbers are more important than people.

In accounting, employees are treated as an expense but great leaders know better. They know people are powerful assets that represent the future results of a company. They see their team as an important resource that needs to be led properly to maximize performance. They understand their team will be at their best when they are loved, appreciated, respected, engaged, and acknowledged.

THE SIMPLE ACT
OF APPRECIATION

Great leaders aren't afraid to love their teams.
– Donald Miller

As CEO, I was out in our factory and noticed our company's top mechanical engineer working on a drill press. He was modifying parts so they could be used in production. He had been there all morning reworking these parts because we had a big customer order that had to go out. It wasn't his job, but he did it anyway because he cared deeply about the success of our company.

As a leader, I couldn't just walk by and ignore his efforts. I stopped and talked to him. I told him how much I appreciated him and the work he was doing. He didn't have to be standing at a drill press all morning working on those production parts but there he was. I had to acknowledge his extra efforts.

The problem with most leaders, however, is they miss these opportunities. Most leaders are sequestered in their offices and oblivious to what's happening with their teams. They are unaware of the extra efforts their best employees are doing every day. These employees are left feeling overworked, overwhelmed, and underappreciated. And, underappreciated employees leave companies.

A study by *OfficeTeam* found that 66% of employees said they would "likely leave their job if they didn't feel appreciated." That number jumps to 76% for millennials. Not feeling appreciated is the leading reason why people leave companies. Yet, many managers still make little effort to show their appreciation.

One of the more frustrating things I see in leaders today is a negative or indifferent attitude towards people. Many choose a career in leadership who don't comprehend the significant daily impact they have on their teams. Most of these leaders find they are less effective because they lack a people-focused mindset. This is because leadership is inherently a people business.

The entire role of a leader is to motivate a team of people towards accomplishing an objective. Great leaders know this and they know it's important to show appreciation. They also know people are messy. People have issues, problems, emotions, quirks, hang-ups, baggage, and can be unpredictable. A great leader can see past the flaws, love their people, and motivate them to do great things. You can't be a great leader if you don't love people.

Donald Miller, founder and CEO of *StoryBrand*, a company that helps businesses clarify their marketing message, sees it the same way. I like his thoughts on this subject as he reflects on the culture he built at his company. One of the core values he put in place was to "make his employees' dreams come true by serving clients faithfully." I thought it was interesting that he purposely intertwined serving customers with the dreams of his employees. In his view, loving your employees and showing appreciation means helping them reach their full potential.

Miller credits the growth of his company to the "secret ingredient" of love. Things changed at his company when they started to live out these core values. As he loved and respected his employees, they loved each other and they worked as a team to better serve customers. He built a culture of respect with a foundation in love.

He has two fundamental rules which have helped him create a culture of love and respect:

1. Hire people who are better, smarter, and faster than you.
2. Never mess with their hearts.

If you're a leader, you have a profound impact on the lives and careers of the people working for you. You need to be patient with their flaws and take time to truly appreciate their contributions. The biggest problem with employee engagement in most companies today is that employees feel their bosses don't appreciate them. Imagine how they will react when they see their boss truly cares.

Putting Employees
Ahead of Customers

Clients do not come first. Employees come first. If you take care of your employees, they will take care of the clients.
– Richard Branson

The best leaders put customers first, right? Not if you are Richard Branson, J. Willard Marriott, Jim Goodnight, or Stephen Covey. They put employees first.

Take a look at these quotes:

- *Take care of your people and they will take care of your customers.* – J. Willard Marriott
- *Treat employees like they make a difference and they will.* – Jim Goodnight
- *Always treat your employees exactly as you want them to treat your best customers.* – Stephen Covey

What these leaders know is that when you take care of your employees, they will take care of your customers. Employees who are respected, appreciated, and are given the chance to grow and thrive will go the extra mile for customers.

Consider the fast food chain, Chick-fil-A. I love their chicken sandwiches and on top of that, I know I'll have a good experience at their restaurants. I always find Chick-fil-A restaurants are clean, the food is good, and the service is fast and friendly. They stand in stark contrast to their fast-food rivals which are filled with apathetic employees attempting a half-hearted effort to make me a subpar meal. I'd rather go to Chick-fil-A than any of their competitors – and I'm not the only one.

Chick-fil-A has the highest revenue per restaurant of any fast-food chain in the U.S., according to *QSR* magazine. An average Chick-fil-A location creates more than three times the revenue of a similar KFC restaurant. Despite having only 1,950 restaurants in the U.S., Chick-fil-A generates more overall revenue than rivals who have twice as many locations, including KFC, Arby's, Pizza Hut, and Domino's. What's even more amazing is that they create this volume of business while being closed every Sunday.

Chick-fil-A has mastered the art of customer service – they simply crush the competition. Chick-fil-A has been ranked #1 in restaurant customer service in the *American Customer Satisfaction Index* for the past three years. They consistently receive high marks for cleanliness, fast service, good food, and hardworking employees who care.

Their employees are simply the best in the business and I was surprised to learn they are paid nearly the same as other fast-food workers. According to *Glassdoor*, Chick-fil-A pays hourly employees on average only $0.46 more an hour than their competitors. If it's not the pay, how does this small fast-food chain create a customer-focused workforce that dominates the competition? The answer is they put employees ahead of customers.

At Chick-fil-A, people are the priority. Even though the hourly pay is similar, Chick-fil-A invests heavily in other areas. Employees are provided extensive training in restaurant operations and there are leadership and career advancement opportunities which are unmatched in the industry. Chick-fil-A's founder Truett Cathy was fond of saying, "We aren't in the chicken business; we are in the people business." Local store owners are encouraged to learn the *dreams of their teams* and help them fulfill them.

As a result, employees are treated more like family. Chick-fil-A owners work to help employees reach their dreams by providing leadership training, academic scholarships, and even paying for classes in unrelated skills like photography and dance. If an employee's family member is sick, they will provide food, encouragement, and support. They'll even supply meals to the hospital staff treating one of their staff members. Kevin Moss, a Chick-fil-A store manager for more than 20 years, told *Business Insider* in a 2016 interview, "I've found people are more motivated and respond better when you care about them."

The success of Chick-fil-A demonstrates that employees who are respected, appreciated, and are given the chance to grow and thrive will always go the extra mile for customers.

At my company, *Peak Demand*, we do the same. We have nine guiding principles. The first is, *We create a cul-*

ture of respect where employees are safe, they love to come to work, and they are empowered to make decisions for our customers. We may not always get it right, but we work hard every day to create and maintain a positive environment for our employees. The result is a workplace that feels more like a family than a corporation. Managers and employees respect each other, have fun, and everyone works hard as a team to satisfy our customers.

As you look at your work environment, what are the written or unwritten priorities? Who is more important – customers or employees? Richard Branson has been incredibly successful as an entrepreneur and business leader. His priorities are clear: Employees first, customers second, and shareholders third. It seems to work well for him. He explains that happy employees take care of customers and happy customers purchase more goods and services, which keeps the shareholders happy. Branson says, "In the end, shareholders do well, the customers do better, and [our] staff remains happy."

HAVING YOUR EMPLOYEE'S BACK

A good manager is a man who isn't worried about his own career but rather the careers of those who work for him.
– Hendry Stuart Mackenzie Burns

I had spent thousands of dollars of the company's money to get to this point. It was my first trip to the high-power test lab and I was nervous. I was the lead mechanical engineer on a project to design a new electrical apparatus that would be safer than anything available on the market. It would be a breakthrough if we succeeded.

I ran all the calculations. I was confident we would pass the test but I was worried our design might not survive the initial shock wave. An electrical shock of 15,000 volts is violent and, despite my calculations, I knew anything could go wrong. I spent the morning getting everything ready for the first test. By noon, it was go-time. There was no backing down.

Less than one second after the fault current was applied, my worst fears were realized. The gear exploded violently. Parts flew off in every direction. It wasn't just a failure – it was an absolute disaster. I had failed spectacularly.

I walked over to the test bay and surveyed the scene. The product was completely destroyed. There was nothing left but a smoking carcass and the smell of melted copper. I knew I had to call my boss and I knew it wouldn't be good. I would probably lose my job for this. I was discouraged. My days in design engineering were probably over.

I returned to the control room and called my boss. I explained what had happened. Expecting the worst, I was shocked at his response. He said to me, "Do you know why it failed?" My answer was *yes*. He then asked, "Do you know how to fix it?" Again, my answer was also *yes*. Without any emotion, he said, "Well, get back here and get the redesign done so you can return to the lab."

I knew right then my boss had my back. Instead of chastising me, he had encouraged me. Instead of losing my job, he had given me a new assignment. My respect for him skyrocketed. After that interaction, I knew I had a good boss and I wanted to make him proud. And I did. I returned to the lab a short month later and passed every test. We were the first to the market with this new technology.

This happened to me more than 20 years ago and I can still remember exactly how I felt that day. I felt empowered knowing I had a boss who would stand behind me even if I made a mistake. Unfortunately, many bosses don't understand the power of supporting their employees. Too many bosses won't back up their team members when bad things happen. As soon as anything casts a shadow on the leader, they abandon their people. They don't want to get in trouble themselves. They are looking out for their own careers. They walk away and let the employee take the fall.

This is the worst type of boss. When something goes wrong, they immediately leave employees hanging – or worse, they throw them under the bus. These bosses want all the glory but they don't want to take any blame for failures. What's worse is that everyone in the organization knows this and it deeply affects the culture.

When employees know they have a boss that won't back them up if anything bad happens, they stop taking chances. They stop trying new things. They stop pushing the envelope of what's possible. They're afraid to fail and that fear grinds the organization to a halt. The organization becomes stagnant and good people start looking for other opportunities.

I will never forget the kindness of that boss. He put my career ahead of his own. I'm sure his reputation suffered for the delays and expense but he never mentioned anything to me. He knew I was doing something that hadn't been done before and there was a chance for failure. He stood behind me and motivated me to get back up again and keep going. In the end, the product was a huge success. We received several patents, awards, and industry recognition for our work. We successfully leapfrogged the competition and introduced a new ground-breaking technology. Our product became the gold standard for safety and the orders soon followed. The company was enormously successful because one leader had my back.

The Importance of Respect

A bad manager can take a good staff and destroy it, causing the best employees to flee and the remainder to lose all motivation. – Unknown

Disengaged employees can be the death of a company. Employees who dislike their jobs, watch the clock, or put the absolute minimum effort into their daily activities can kill the performance of a business. The problem is significant. According to the *State of the American Workplace* report by *Gallup*, 70% of employees are currently disengaged at work, costing U.S. companies more than $450 billion in lost productivity. They also found that leaders play a critical role in the level of engagement.

"Employee engagement" has become one of the latest corporate buzzwords, with 78% of business leaders saying it is both an urgent and important priority, per the multinational accounting firm *Deloitte*. Companies have tried a range of techniques to improve their level of engagement but, according to *Gallup*, the percentage of engaged employees has not changed significantly in the past five years.

What if the solution to the problem were simple? What

if, as a leader, you could change just one thing to create an actively engaged workforce? Research has shown there is a simple answer and it is related to the level of respect you give to your employees.

A study by HR consulting company *Psychometrics Canada* indicates that employee engagement directly affects the production and efficiency of an organization. Actively engaged employees provide real, tangible benefits to organizations. The study found 39% of engaged employees showed a willingness to do more than expected, 27% exhibited higher productivity, and 13% reported better working relationships.

They also learned the most significant driver to create and sustain an environment of strong employee engagement was the company's leadership. More than 80% of survey respondents indicated that leaders and managers were primarily responsible for the level of employee engagement.

When asked what leaders could do to improve employee engagement, survey respondents all pointed to one word: *respect*. Employees want to be respected by the people they work for. They want leaders who are considerate, communicate clear expectations, listen to employees' opinions, and provide regular feedback.

The truth is that many managers have never been formally trained in leadership. They are promoted because of their education, technical ability, or past performance. Because of this, they may not fully understand how critical their actions are in creating and sustaining an environment of employee engagement.

Paul Marciano, author of *Carrots and Sticks Don't Work: Build a Culture of Employee Engagement with the Principles of RESPECT*, points out seven simple ways in which leaders can show respect to their employees:

Recognition. Thanking employees and acknowledging their contributions on a regular basis.

Empowerment. Providing employees with the appropriate resources, training, information, and authority to get the job done.

Supportive Feedback. Giving regular performance feedback — both positive and corrective.

Partnering. Fostering a collaborative working environment where employees' opinions are sought out and considered.

Expectation setting. Establishing and communicating clear performance goals and objectives.

Consideration. Demonstrating genuine thoughtfulness, empathy, and kindness.

Trust. Demonstrating faith and belief in employees' skills, abilities, and decisions.

As leaders, we can directly affect the amount of employee engagement in our companies by our actions. We can lead by example by showing respect to our employees at every level. It is also critical to find, train, and promote managers and supervisors who can also demonstrate these skills on a regular basis.

As disengaged employees can be the death of a company, engaged employees can breathe life back into a company. It's our duty as leaders to create an environment where employees are respected, engaged, and excited to be part of the team. The result will be real, tangible improvements in the company's morale and performance.

SHOWING YOU CARE

Nobody cares how much you know, until
they know how much you care.
– Often attributed to Theodore Roosevelt

Former Dallas Cowboys and Miami Dolphins coach Jimmy Johnson probably said it best: "The difference between ordinary and extraordinary is that little extra." This is especially true in leadership. Getting the business fundamentals right is critical for success, but how you treat your people is that little "extra" that can truly inspire an organization.

The problem is that too many leaders don't see this. *Harvard Business Review* conducted a study of 20,000 people around the world and found that 54% of employees felt their leaders didn't treat them with respect on a regular basis. They surmised their bosses didn't care.

Christine Porath, a professor at Georgetown University, researched this subject in greater detail. She asked managers to describe why they didn't treat their employees with respect. She found that:

- More than 60% of managers said they were *too busy* to take the time to be nice.

- Another 29% claimed they were just *acting like other managers* in their organization.
- And 4% admitted they are *intentionally disrespectful* to employees because they knew they could get away with it.

This lack of respect and civility has a negative impact on employee engagement. A *Harvard Business Review* study found that showing respect and caring is more important to employee engagement than any other factor. Employees who said their boss cared were 55% more engaged.

The truth is, it's not difficult or time-consuming to display genuine care for your employees. It's that little "extra" you can do to create a positive work environment where people genuinely want to do their best every day. In close to 30 years as a leader, I found these 10 simple activities can make a significant difference in employee engagement:

Be present. Never underestimate the power of your presence. You need to be there. You need to walk around. You can't lead your company from behind your desk. Employees need to see you and you need to see them.

Focus on them. When engaging employees, remember it's not about you. Ask them questions. Find out about them. Find out what's on their minds. Most corporate communication is top-down but when you talk with employees, there is opportunity for a more interactive dialogue.

Be polite. It doesn't take any extra time to say *please* and *thank you*, and to acknowledge that you appreciate someone's effort.

Don't forget to smile. As a leader, you are being watched daily and your attitude is contagious. Even if you are having a bad day, force yourself to be positive and smile when engaging employees.

Give them your full attention. Nothing says disrespect more than ignoring an employee. When it comes to employee interactions, never multitask. Stop what you are doing and acknowledge them. It's acceptable to let them know you need a minute to wrap up what you are doing but then put it away and give them 100% of your attention.

Send thank you notes. A simple note thanking an employee for his or her extra effort helps reinforce the right employee behaviors. It shows you care.

Send get well cards. I keep a stack of "get well" cards in my desk to send to employees who are sick or having surgery. It's a simple thing that shows you care about them as individuals.

Attend funerals. Rudy Giuliani famously said, "Weddings are optional, but funerals are mandatory." I try to attend the funerals of family members of my direct reports and those of employees or recent retirees. This is a critical way to show you care.

Welcome new employees. I once had a boss who sent a large basket of cookies and snacks to my home after he hired me. In it was a note that said, "I'm looking forward to all the great things I know you will do." It was a simple gesture that I will never forget.

Promote a culture of respect. It is important to select

leaders who share your desire to show respect to employees. The primary reason employees leave companies is poor leadership of front-line managers. Make sure your leadership team knows the importance you place on respect by promoting those who display the right behaviors.

To be an extraordinary leader, you have to love people. You need to do the little "extra" things to show you care, you are listening, and you recognize your employees' efforts. Most leaders claim they don't have enough time to show respect to their employees yet they seem to find time to deal with the aftermath of poor employee morale and engagement.

I challenge you to try these 10 simple activities and see if they make a difference in your organization.

CELEBRATING EMPLOYEES

*I'm convinced that celebrating wins does more to
clarify the vision than anything else.*
– Andy Stanley

My father is awesome. As a retired high-voltage electrician, he loves the fact that I run a business that manufactures electrical products. He has always been interested in what I am doing with the company. He is especially attentive to the little things I do for my employees. What's even better is he suggests ideas from time to time. The other day, he made me laugh.

"You should implement Wiener Wednesdays," he said. "Get all the employees together on Wednesday afternoon and have hot dogs. It would be good for morale and to build up the team."

Despite the funny name, it's a brilliant idea.

I'm a huge proponent of doing the extra things to celebrate employees. It's one of the best things you can do for morale. I have had the honor of leading nine different manufacturing businesses in my career. I've found that honoring employees, celebrating successes, and treating people with respect leads to improved job satisfaction, morale, and engagement.

Over the years, I've done many things to celebrate employees. Some of them were big and required significant planning; others were small, just a simple way to say *thank you*. Regardless of the size, each conveyed a message: "You are important, respected, and appreciated."

Here are some examples of things I've done over the years. It's not a complete list but just a sampling of some of the things you can do for people. I hope it inspires you to think of new ways to honor and celebrate your team.

Lobsterfest. During an all-employee meeting, I once promised a factory workforce lobster dinner if we reached 1,000,000 hours of safe work, something that had never been done before at this operation. When we hit the milestone, we had a huge celebration that included steaks and flying 400 live lobsters in from Maine.

Family day. In one business, we invited employees and their families to an annual family day at a large amusement park. Employees spent the day in the park with their families and then gathered for a group lunch in the pavilion, where we held a raffle and gave out gifts.

Fridays on the floor. At several of my plants, the first Friday of the month was reserved for the management team to work on the shop floor. This gave us a chance to get to know people better and to learn ways to make things easier for them.

Open house. Over the years, I have held factory open houses for the friends and family of employees. These were fun events with food, activities, and a chance for employees to show off where they work and what they did.

Letters home. One of the things I like to do is send a letter to the home of an employee who has done something above and beyond. It's more powerful than just giving it to them at work. When the letter is sent home, the employee's family can see it as well.

Buddy the Elf. At one business, I had the annual Christmas tradition to dress up like Buddy the Elf. I would climb on the back of an electric maintenance cart with another manager dressed as Santa. We would ride around the plant and give out candy to all the employees.

Wall of fame. I started a tradition at one plant of hanging pictures in the lobby of employees who received a patent and those who had qualified as a Six Sigma Black Belt. Every customer coming to our plant knew who our rock stars were.

Veterans Day. As a veteran myself, I have always made a point to celebrate Veterans Day with all our veteran employees. It usually involves a small celebration with a cake, a gift, and a ceremony to replace the American flag in front of the plant with a new one.

Team pride. At one business, we had employees hang flags of their favorite sports team throughout the offices. We also had jersey days when the employees were encouraged to wear sports team jerseys to work.

Swag. People like to belong and everyone loves logo-wear. Getting a shirt, a cup, or a hat with a company logo gives you a sense of pride and belonging. I love seeing employees wearing shirts they have received as gifts over the years. I've given out backpacks, coffee mugs, water bottles, jackets, beer glasses, and even coolers to say *thank you* to employees over the years.

This list is just a small sampling of some of the fun things I've done to celebrate and honor employees. As a leader, I want to create an environment that is both safe and fun so that people actually enjoy coming to work each day. I believe in a workplace where talented employees are respected and empowered, and where they are provided opportunities to fully serve the needs of our customers. In truth, honoring and respecting employees is not difficult or expensive but the payoffs are incredible.

For those who were wondering, I did take my father's advice and we had our first "Wiener Wednesday" cookout.

Doing Something
Memorable

The manner of giving is worth more than the gift.
– Pierre Corneille

When the company I co-founded celebrated its first anniversary, I wanted to do something special. As you can imagine, the first year of any new company is especially difficult because you are building everything from the ground up. Our first nine employees had to endure challenges that will never be seen by future employees. That makes them very special.

Because of that, I wanted to do something unique to thank them for their extraordinary efforts. The challenge, of course, was that we were a young company and our resources were going towards payroll, factory equipment, inventory, and travel to visit customers. I needed to create something significant that didn't cost a lot.

It only took a quick walk around our offices to understand what is meaningful to people. You can see the same in your business. Employees decorate their individual work areas with things that have significance or meaning to them. If you look beyond the personal items to the work-related objects, you see the treasures employees keep to remind them of important times in their careers. They are tokens of the past proudly on display.

In my case, I have a photo signed by all the employees of my first manufacturing business. It is my most sacred work treasure because it reminds me of all the good times I had leading this amazing team.

If you want to give a memorable gift, something that will become a special treasure to your employees, consider these five principles:

It should be an exceptional event. It should represent a significant achievement. Gifts and celebrations should be special. They should represent something of importance to the company or employee. Celebrating and giving gifts too often minimize the impact.

It should fit on a desk. It should be something that can become a memento. Giving a gift card, a travel mug, or a T-shirt is great but it's not likely to become a treasured token. Pick something that is unique and can be displayed in the employee's work area without taking up space.

It should be personal. A gift with the company logo is nice but your gift will mean more if it is personalized. Something signed by the team or with the employee's name and accomplishment will mean more.

It should show the employee is part of something special. As humans, we like to belong. Giving a gift that shows the employee belongs to a special or elite group will have more meaning. A patent plaque or a Six Sigma Black Belt award shows the employee has achieved a significant milestone in his or her career.

It should reinforce your principles. Keep in mind that the employee receiving the gift is not the only one who will be affected. Other employees should notice the gift and understand the significance. They should be motivated to try to achieve similar success.

In my case, I decided to give each of our employees a rock carved with the company logo and the phrase "The Founding Nine." When I presented them, I said there would only be nine of these rocks ever made and they were the only ones to get them. I chose a rock because it represented the solid foundation with which we would build the company. I also wanted each rock to be different to represent the varied strengths each person brought to the team.

Giving a memorable gift is easier than you think. Walk around your offices and learn what your employees truly treasure. You will be amazed at what you see. Following these five simple principles will help you give gifts that will become your employees' treasured tokens.

GIVING INTANGIBLE GIFTS

I've learned that people will forget what you said, people will forget what you did, but people will never forget how you made them feel. – Maya Angelou

As you think back on your career, what gifts did you receive from the people you worked for? I'm not talking about physical gifts but the things they did that left a lasting impact on you.

A study by *Glassdoor* found that 66% of employees believe their direct managers had an impact on their careers; 52% indicated the impact was positive while 20% said it was negative. The challenge as leaders is that, whether we like it or not, we leave a lasting legacy on the people who follow us.

In looking back at all the leaders I have worked for, I can recall a number of good gifts that have had a lasting effect on me:

The gift of trust. As a junior officer assigned to my first submarine, I had a commanding officer who regularly chose me for the toughest assignments. Even though I was filled with self-doubt, he told me he trusted me and that I would do a good job. That trust gave me confidence.

The gift of appreciation. I once had a boss who sent a huge basket of cookies and snacks to my home after he hired me. In it was a note that said, "I'm looking forward to all the great things I know you will do." It was a simple gesture that said he appreciated me as a person even before I started work.

The gift of faith. The leader that selected me to run my first manufacturing plant chose me for the job, even though I had never run a manufacturing operation before. His action told me that he had faith in my abilities and I worked hard to prove him right.

The gift of support. When I was going through a career transition, I had several former bosses who went out of their way to provide support and advice through the whole process. Their support during a stressful time was exactly what I needed to make a successful transition.

The gift of encouragement. As a young design engineer, I had a major failure of a new product at a test lab, costing my company thousands of dollars. I had to call my boss to give him the bad news. Instead of a reprimand, he encouraged me to learn as much as I could about the failure, improve the product, and to get back to the lab.

The gift of recognition. I have had a number of bosses who have selected me to receive awards or have recognized me publicly for my actions. In most cases, it was a total surprise. Although I didn't work for the recognition, it was nice to get that type of positive feedback.

The gift of a challenge. I once had a boss challenge a business plan I developed. Even though I had created a solid plan, he asked one simple question which changed everything. He simply said, "This is great, but what haven't you thought of that could double your business?" That challenge was the catalyst that changed my entire thinking and business model.

As you look back at your time as a leader, think about the gifts you have been giving. Have they been good gifts? What is the lasting legacy you are leaving for the people who work for you? What can you do differently going forward?

LISTENING TO EMPLOYEES

Leaders must recognize that the key to success and growth is getting employees to tell you what's really going on.
– Vineet Nayar

What if you could know what your employees were thinking? What if you could see the company through their eyes? How would your leadership efforts change if you knew what truly motivated your team?

Believe it or not, understanding your team and how to lead them effectively is easier than you think. The problem is most leaders don't spend enough time with employees, really listening to them.

Listening to employees is a critical skill to master in order to become a more insightful and effective leader. This seems simple but it's often overlooked. Most leaders spend their day in a bubble. They find themselves surrounded by people who see the company exactly as they do. Getting out of the office and spending time listening to employees will help you break out of that bubble and give you a different perspective.

Here are four ways that listening to employees improves your skills as a leader:

You create relationships. When you spend time listening to employees, you get to know them and they get to know you. In the process, you build mutual respect. You build a relationship. As you learn more about their passions and challenges, you understand how to lead them more effectively. They will also get to know you and the reasons behind your actions.

You face reality. Listening to employees gives you a unique perspective. You discover how things are really going. Employees can be brutally honest, which is why many leaders avoid this activity. If you are going to lead effectively, you need to confront reality and address the challenges your team is facing.

You uncover common themes. As you listen to employees, you discover common themes. These are small pieces of a narrative that tell a bigger story. You might find that employees are having a problem with one of your supervisors or a new piece of software. You may uncover a common customer complaint or lingering production bottleneck. Spending time with employees gives you access to real information that is often filtered out in a traditional command-and-control management structure.

You build a team. When leaders and employees spend time together, they become more aware that they are on the same team. It's easy to blame someone you don't know or understand for your problems. Listening to employees can help eliminate the "us and them" mindset. When we do that, we can better focus our attention on customers, the competition, and getting better as a company.

Some of the best leadership insights are found in the breakroom, not the boardroom. If you find yourself surrounded by people who see the company exactly as you do, you probably need to break out of your bubble and go spend time listening to employees. This simple act will help you build critical relationships, confront reality, uncover common concerns, and build a stronger team.

Communicating
Face-to-Face

Do more listening than talking; talk more about them than about you. – Roy T. Bennett

Have you ever had one of those bosses who was never around? They worked in an office with the door closed, they never came to your work area or location, they spent all their time in meetings, or maybe didn't even know your name? As an employee, it can be incredibly discouraging to have a disengaged boss.

The problem is that most leaders don't understand the power of their presence. They don't understand the importance of face-to-face communications. This is probably why, according to the *State of the American Workplace* report by *Gallup*, 70% of employees are disengaged with their company. Employees need to see you and you need to see them.

So, why is it important that employees see their boss on a regular basis? Let me suggest five simple reasons, especially in this time of decentralized offices and remote locations, that leaders need to be face-to-face with their employees:

You ensure proper communication. Robert Whipple, CEO of *Leadergrow,* an organization dedicated to the development of leaders, wrote about this in an article called "Face to Face." In it, he refers to the old *UCLA* study that showed that only 7% of what is understood is from words – the rest comes from facial expressions and the tone of your voice. He suggests that in a time of decentralized offices, an overreliance on texts and e-mails will cause your communications to suffer. You must see your employees face-to-face to ensure your message is understood.

You see what is really going on. As a leader, you need to get out of your office and go to where the value-added work is being done. Too many times, leaders make decisions based on what they think is going on. Unless you spend time with your employees face-to-face, there will be a significant gap between reality and your assumptions on reality.

You learn new things. There is a rich and useful world of "tribal knowledge" to be discovered. The collective wisdom of your employees is incredible but you need to be present to learn about it. Your employees know what works and what doesn't. They know where the real problems and opportunities are. Spending time with employees gives you a new perspective.

They see you as approachable. Every boss likes to be viewed as approachable but what do your actions tell your employees? Do you work with your office door shut? Do you walk through the office looking down at the floor? Demonstrate you are approachable by getting out of your office with the purpose of saying *good morning* to your employees. If you have remote employees, spend a week working at their location so they see you. The more approachable you appear, the more likely they will open up and talk to you.

They see you as part of the team. Too often, leaders think they are more important than their employees. The truth is, more value-added activity is occurring with your employees than with you. You may be the coach, but they are on the field making it happen every day. By being present and showing up to talk to your employees, they see you as an important part of the team, not just a name on the bottom of an e-mail.

They see you as the company. Whether you like it or not, your employees see you as the company. If you are distant and disengaged as a leader, they will be the same with your company. The truth is that front-line leaders trump CEOs when it comes to employee engagement. A *Harvard Business Review* study found that 73% of employees said front-line managers were vitally important to achieving a high level of employee engagement. If you want engaged employees, you need to be an engaged leader.

The fact that 70% of employees in the U.S. are disengaged at work tells me that, as leaders, we still have a lot of work to do to improve our leadership skills. One of the most important skills is simply to spend time with your employees face-to-face. Too often, leaders are disconnected and disengaged. Being present ensures you are communicating properly, you face reality, you become more approachable, and you foster an environment of employ-ee engagement. In the end, getting out of your office and spending time with your employees will make you a better leader.

Understanding the
Power of Your Presence

*Leadership is about making others better as a
result of your presence and making sure that
impact lasts in your absence.*
– Sheryl Sandberg

Never underestimate the power of your presence and how it affects your team. As a leader, everyone is watching you. If you come late to meetings, everyone knows. If you don't wear your personal protective equipment in the factory, everyone sees it. If you leave early, your team is keenly aware. What you do speaks louder than what you say. The truth is, your minimal acceptable standard of performance is often the maximum level for your team so your actions need to be carefully considered.

A great example of the power of presence came several years back when I took over the leadership of a manufacturing plant with around 200 employees. As I walked through the operation on my first plant tour with the leadership team, I saw a forklift coming towards me from a perpendicular aisle. It was a blind aisle and I looked up and noticed there wasn't a safety mirror mounted at the intersection. It was a safety problem that needed to be addressed. I made a mental note of it but didn't say anything to the team.

The next morning as I walked around the plant on my own, I went over to the same intersection. To my surprise, someone had mounted a safety mirror in the exact spot where I had been looking. I never mentioned anything to the leadership team but they clearly saw where I looked and they knew I had just found a safety problem. They addressed it before I even mentioned it.

I learned three important lessons from this experience:

As a leader, people are watching you. They notice the little things you do, what you say, and how you say it. They noticed I looked up and saw something was wrong. Even though I hadn't said a word, they knew I was concerned so they took action without being told.

Your minimal acceptable standard of performance is often the maximum level for your team. If I had walked through that intersection without noticing the problem, it might never have been addressed. As leaders, if we walk by a problem and don't acknowledge it, our people will think it's acceptable. As an example, I never walk by a piece of trash at work because I know that just stopping and picking it up sends a clear message.

If you want to signal your priorities, you need to get out of your office. That quick walk around the plant signaled to the leadership team that I wanted to see what was going on. Noticing the missing safety mirror showed that safety was important to me. The only way you will be exposed to what is really going on in your business is to get out of your office and go to where the value is being added.

Your presence is powerful and what you do is impactful. Never miss the chance to communicate your priorities by your actions.

The Problem with Busyness

Often he who does too much does too little.
– Italian Proverb

"The managers of this company just don't care." That was the feedback I had just received from one of my production workers and I was trying to process it. I had worked hard with my leadership team to get them to engage with employees. I couldn't understand why we weren't seeing better results.

The feedback had come during my monthly "birthday meeting." As plant manager, I met with a different group of employees each month to get their thoughts on how the business was going. They were called birthday meetings because employees who had a birthday in that month were invited. I was leading a small manufacturing operation with 160 employees. Each meeting had about 10-15 employees. This month's feedback was hard to swallow.

I pushed for more details. I wanted to understand why this employee thought our managers didn't care. He talked specifically about one of the managers: "Every time I see him, his head is down or he is rushing to another meeting." The person he was talking about was my best manager. He cared deeply for his team and the factory overall. He was a good leader. I couldn't believe what I was hearing!

Later that day, I spoke to the manager. I wanted to get his perspective and what he said was equally eye-opening. He told me that he was very busy – so busy, in fact, that he kept his head down when walking through the plant. He told me, "I don't want to get distracted or get pulled into a long conversation. I have a lot to do and I want to get it all done." To my surprise, I realized that my leadership team was so busy that they didn't have time to lead.

This happens far too often in organizations. Leaders with good intentions take on far too many activities. They fail to properly delegate tasks and, in the end, they fail to lead their teams properly. They are too busy and employees feel like they don't care.

If you feel like you are too busy to lead, step back and conduct this simple exercise:

Track what you do each day. Keep a notebook of your daily activities for a week and see where you are spending all your time. In most cases, you will be surprised by the results.

Identify those things that only you can do as a leader. Look through your daily activities and mark those that only you can do. These are critical tasks like planning, directing, evaluating, and interacting with employees.

Identify activities that you can delegate. Determine which activities can be delegated. These are actions that can be done by others. They are time-consuming tasks that others are more suited to complete.

Oftentimes we confuse busyness with usefulness or effectiveness. In the case of leaders, being busy can actually be detrimental to our most important role. Leadership is the act of influencing a group of people to accomplish a goal. If we spend all our time completing tasks, we miss out on the important job of influencing. While you are rushing to a meeting or spending all day working on e-mails, you are missing out on the opportunity to interact with your team. And worse yet, they think you don't care.

The simple truth is, when you find ways to stop being so busy, you become a better leader.

THE ABSENT LEADER

When there is no leader, or when the leader is silent, chaos takes over. – Jon S. Rennie

While most people identify micromanagement as the worst leadership style, there is another type of boss who is equally destructive to an organization – the absent leader.

This is the type of boss who is distant, aloof, or so busy that he or she doesn't perform the basic duties of a leader. Leadership is about being present. It's about setting the direction for your team and accomplishing goals. It's also about resolving issues and conflicts when they arise.

Absent leaders create a situation where employees each do what they think is best for the organization. Most people care about their company and they want it to succeed but when the leader steps away, there is not one unifying person guiding the organization. Everybody decides what's best to do. In the absence of clear direction, the organization will drift further from its mission.

The other problem is that one individual might choose to go one way and another person goes a different way. This results in the organization getting pulled in many different directions and creates internal conflict, unnecessary debate, and arguments – which wastes precious time and resources.

Another example of this is rumors. When a leader doesn't adequately explain what's happening in an organization, especially during times of change, rumors will get started. People will speculate on what's going to happen. These rumors will run through an organization and do nothing but create worry and waste time, energy, and resources.

There are three ways to avoid becoming an absent leader:

Be present. Be there for your team. Listen to what's going on in the organization. Walk around the workplace and be seen. Be alert for rumors and internal debates. Understand where people may be wasting energy and where divisiveness exists.

Lead the organization. Set the vision and the objectives. Establish clear boundaries and expectations. Let your team know what the priorities are. Be there to resolve conflicts and make hard decisions. Don't shy away from your responsibilities.

Don't stand for chaos. It's the leader's job to build a stable, smooth-running business. Chaos should always be the exception and not the rule. It's good to have debate and discussion but allowing constant infighting and arguments only wastes the time and energy of an organization. It does not put you closer to your goal.

Take a look at your company and see what's going on. If there is chaos and confusion, you are probably not doing your job; you might be an absent leader. You may have the leadership title and the corner office but you are not leading your team, and that can be devastating to your organization.

STOP BEING A JERK

Leaders who don't listen will eventually be surrounded
by people who have nothing to say.
– Andy Stanley

In more than 30 years of work, I wish I could say I have never worked for a bad manager. The truth is, I've had a few terrible bosses. Part of the problem is a lack of leadership training. Most managers today have received little or no training in leading people. The other part of the problem is that some people are just jerks. Amy Osmond Cook wrote about this in an article called "Are You a Jerk? 10 Questions to Ask Yourself." In it, she provides a self-assessment to check your level of "jerkness." Applying this thinking, I created a list for you to evaluate your leadership style to see if you might be a jerk at work. Here are 10 characteristics of bosses who are jerks:

They won't give others their full attention. A sure sign a boss is a jerk is if they are more interested in their phones, computers, or paperwork than the people who work for them. Great bosses stop what they are doing to listen to their people. Jerks don't.

They make promises with no intention to keep them. Bad bosses make false promises to get what they want from people. They tell employees what they want to hear with no intentions of keeping their word. Great bosses meet their commitments to their people. Jerks don't.

They keep all information close to the vest. Great bosses trust people and they are open and honest with communications. Bad bosses don't trust anyone and they rarely share information for fear it may be used against them. Bosses who intentionally keep their people in the dark are jerks.

They stay isolated. The closed office door is a sure sign they want to be left alone and a pretty good indication they may be jerks. Poor bosses stay isolated, they rarely visit their employees, and they avoid spending time with the workforce. Bosses who are jerks never visit their employees' work areas and have no idea what their employees do for the company.

They care more about their careers than the company. Bosses who are jerks make every decision based on how it will look for their careers. They care only for themselves and are willing to allow bad things to happen to other departments or employees if it makes them look better. Great leaders put the company and their people ahead of themselves.

They don't show respect for others' time. Bosses who are jerks are constantly late to meetings, frequently reschedule appointments, and keep employees in discussions long after the end of their shifts. Great leaders treat their people and their time with respect. Jerks only care about themselves.

They don't trust you to make decisions. Jerks tend to micromanage and don't trust their team members to make decisions. Great leaders inspire and empower people because they trust them. Bosses who say they can't trust any of their employees are probably jerks.

They don't give you unfiltered access to senior management. Because jerks are primarily motivated by their careers, they spend a lot of time controlling the messages to their supervisors. They fear employees will mess up their charade and reveal the truth. Managers who keep employees away from their bosses are most likely jerks.

They use words like "I" more than "We." There's no "I" in team but there are a lot of them coming from jerks. How they talk to their own bosses will give you an indication of their jerk level. If you lose count of the number of times they say "I" – especially when you know they should be saying "We" – they are probably jerks.

They rarely provide praise but they carefully document all criticism. A clear sign a boss is a jerk is if they put all criticism in writing and rarely praise their employees' work. Putting negative feedback in writing is a sign they are building a case against an employee, likely for termination. Remember, jerks only care about their careers; everyone else can be sacrificed.

If you exhibit two or more of these signs, you might be a jerk but that's OK – there is a cure. It's simple too: Talk to the people who work for you. Ask them for their honest feedback. Ask them where you are coming up short and how you can be a more effective leader. Listening to and taking action on constructive criticism from your employees is a sure sign you are on the road to recovery.

BUILDING AN
UNSTOPPABLE TEAM

The great teams find a way to win. - Allan Ray

Have you ever noticed that there are some teams who just know how to win? Companies that outpace their rivals, sports teams that dominate their competition, or military units that seem to do the impossible. There is something special about these teams that make them unstoppable.

Consider the 2016-2017 New England Patriots in Super Bowl LI. Midway through the third quarter, they were losing 28-3. No other team in Super Bowl history had ever come back from this level of deficit. Despite the odds, quarterback Tom Brady was sure they would win. Later, when asked why he was so confident, he said: "We're in the locker room with each other every day and we know what we're all about. That's what it comes down to. We believe in one another, everyone doing their job."

As leaders, our job is to build and lead our teams. Leading a team is one thing but how do you build a team and make it unstoppable? How do you build a team that will be resilient, persistent, and consistently effective?

Let me suggest that there are four important things to

consider when building an unstoppable team:

Select individuals who have complementary skill sets. This is especially important in small teams. Everyone should have a specific expertise that is required to accomplish the team's objective. Take, for example, Navy Seals. In each team, there are specialists like medics, snipers, explosive technicians, jumpmasters, divemasters, or language experts. Even though there are overlapping skills, the experts are relied on by the team for success in specific areas of the mission. Look at the team you are assembling. Do they have complementary skill sets? Do they have the combined skills to complete the objective?

Select individuals who have achieved a high level of competency. As a former Naval Officer on nuclear submarines, I appreciate the brilliance of the Navy's qualification program. To be promoted or to assume certain duties, you had to go through a rigorous qualification process. This meant everyone you served with had achieved a high level of competency. This established mutual respect across the team and built a high level of trust. You knew your teammate had your back. While more difficult to do in business, you should carefully consider the competency of each team member.

Select individuals who have proved themselves under adversity. Persistent people are extremely valuable to the success of any team. Look for those special employees who can step up and deliver results regardless of the adverse circumstances. Look for people who don't quit and have a proven history of perseverance. Look for the engineer who worked two jobs and went to night school for six years to graduate, the veteran who served two combat tours, or the plant manager who worked his way up from the shop floor. These are the people who are going to make a difference when things get tough.

Select individuals who are unselfish and have a "mission first" mindset. The success of unstoppable teams resides in the singular focus on the mission. "Mission first" employees understand the objective takes priority over individual goals and career aspirations. In the example of Tom Brady, he took a pay cut to allow his team to have the budget to bring in other top talent. This mindset creates a culture where individuals hold each other mutually accountable to the team's goal. There's little room for office politics and egos when the priority is winning.

The objective of leadership is to direct a group of individuals to achieve a common goal. The most important part of that objective is choosing the right people who will make up the team. Selecting employees with the right characteristics, experience, and mindset can make the job of winning easier. Unstoppable teams are uncommon because building a team like this isn't easy. You need to find the right people – employees with complementary skills sets and a high level of competency who have proven themselves under adversity, and who also have a "mission first" mindset.

GETTING THE MOST FROM YOUR TEAM

Success requires greater effort than most employees are prepared to make, however, no more than most are capable of. – Percy Barnevik

I was a 32-year-old engineering manager with virtually no manufacturing experience, but that didn't matter. The company needed a strong leader to take over one of the key manufacturing operations in the division and, because I had demonstrated the ability to get things done, I was asked to lead this business. This was the culture that Percy Barnevik created.

My first job after serving in the U.S. Navy was working for ABB, a global engineering company. Our CEO at the time was the legendary, hard-charging Swede, Percy Barnevik. In 1988, Barnevik created ABB by pulling off the largest European merger at the time, bringing together two engineering powerhouses, ASEA and Brown Boveri Ltd.

What I loved about Barnevik was his bias towards action. He got things done. He was decisive and he expected the same from his employees. The company culture at that time reflected his personality. We moved fast and we fixed it along the way. He knew how to bring out the best of his employees by challenging them to do more.

Barnevik believed in getting the most out of his teams. He created a culture where we challenged each other to do the impossible. It was a company where the status quo was constantly questioned and we worked hard to create new levels of performance.

He understood one of the most important roles of a leader is to set expectations and Barnevik kept his standards very high. He expected strong performance but he also knew that he had to create an environment where employees could take chances and try out new methods and techniques to improve the business.

Here are four things Barnevik did to get the most out of his teams:

Challenging assignments. Barnevik thought good people should be challenged. It was not uncommon for strong-performing employees to be placed in high-profile assignments which were far beyond their proven abilities. This allowed employees to have the opportunity to showcase their skills and provided management with a way to quickly evaluate talent.

Professional development. Barnevik believed in giving employees opportunities to grow professionally. In my time working for him, I attended countless domestic and international training sessions which exposed me to new ideas and helped me further develop my leadership skills.

A forgiving culture. Barnevik pushed decision making to the lowest level and embedded a culture of decisiveness at all levels. He created a culture of speed, decisiveness, and forgiveness. If you made a bad decision, it was not the end of your career. You were expected to fix it and move on. This allowed leaders to try new ideas to improve performance without the constant fear of being fired.

Recognition for high achievement. Barnevik also understood that excellence should be recognized. He had countless programs to acknowledge significant achievement throughout the organization. This created positive feedback for high-performing employees and generated internal competition, which continued to boost performance.

I was fortunate to serve under Percy Barnevik during his time at ABB. Because of the culture he created, I was given the opportunity to lead a manufacturing operation at a young age. The company continued to invest in me and I grew as a business leader. Like many, I thrived in the culture he created where speed, decisiveness, and forgiveness were embraced and high achievement was recognized.

Recognizing and Developing New Leaders

To do great things is difficult; but to
command great things is more difficult.
– Friedrich Nietzsche

I had a great opportunity to teach a session on leadership to a group of graduate students finishing up their International MBA program at the University of South Carolina. My presentation was titled "Leadership Matters – Lessons from the Front Line." The feedback I received was positive but a bit surprising.

The students said the presentation was extremely valuable because it exposed them to the real world of business leadership. They said it was the first time they had a chance to listen to a seasoned executive talking plainly about the challenges of leading people. As it turns out, there are actually no courses on leadership in their program of study.

The sad truth is that most managers today have not received any formal leadership training. Most employees are promoted into leadership positions because of their education, seniority, technical skills, or past performance. Most simply learn leadership "on the job" and many don't have the necessary skills to be a leader. This is probably why there is such a leadership gap in business today.

In fact, the *Gallup* organization reports that 70% of employees remain disengaged at work, a number that has stayed consistent for the past five years. They also found that leadership played the most significant factor in the level of employee engagement. They found that leaders accounted for the largest source of variance in employee engagement across businesses. Their conclusions were clear and disturbing. The lack of great leaders in companies is the primary reason for poor employee engagement.

Even worse, they concluded that great leaders are rare and difficult to find. Their study showed that only one in 10 people possess the talent to lead people. Those 10% have the natural skills and abilities to engage employees, work with customers, retain top talent, and create a high-performance culture.

They also found that an additional 20% of people have some of the characteristics necessary to be a great leader. Those individuals can become great leaders if their company invests in coaching and developmental plans for them. The *Gallup* conclusion was that great leaders are hard to find and most will require coaching and training to reach their full potential.

How can you close the leadership gap in your organization? Let me suggest four areas of focus:

Look for leadership talents and abilities in your employees. Great leaders are hard to find but even harder to detect if you don't actively look for them. You should spend time with your employees looking for those who step up and naturally lead projects or initiatives.

Give potential leaders opportunities to lead. If you have employees with leadership potential, regardless of their seniority or experience, give them an opportunity to run a small project or lead an activity. This will give you an opportunity to validate your assumptions.

Promote leaders based on leadership talents and abilities. It's important to avoid the pitfalls of promoting based on seniority, technical skills, or past performance. According to *Gallup*, only a third of your employees will actually have the talent to be great leaders. Look for leadership talent and abilities first.

Train your leaders like any other discipline. Employees with leadership talent still need coaching and training to become great leaders. Leadership skills are like any other skill. They must be taught, trained, and practiced to reach a high level of proficiency. Since leadership directly drives employee engagement and business performance, leadership training and development should be a top priority.

The *Gallup* study makes a clear case for solving the employee engagement crisis in this country. The solution is simple: We need better leadership. The problem is that great leaders are hard to find and companies today are not doing a good job of identifying, promoting, and developing leadership talent.

As leaders in our organizations, we need to change this. We need to keep a careful eye out for leadership talent in our employees, give potential leaders a chance to lead, promote leaders based on leadership abilities, and develop our leaders through coaching and training. If we place a high value on leadership in our organizations, we can begin to create the culture of employee engagement we so desperately need.

FINDING THE RIGHT LEADERSHIP BALANCE

Leadership is hard. It's a skill. It's a technique.
– Jocko Willink

I once had a boss I secretly nicknamed "TQ" which stood for "Twenty Questions." The reason he earned that name is that every time we met to review the progress of the business he would ask me at least 20 questions about everything I was working on. He micromanaged every aspect of my responsibility and I hated it. It felt like he didn't fully trust my decisions. He was way too involved.

On the other hand, I had a different boss who was completely disengaged. I rarely heard from him unless something went wrong and he never visited my location or met with my teams. He was aloof and disconnected. He had no idea about the daily challenges and successes of our operation. It felt like he didn't care and that our team wasn't important to the company. Both leaders had taken their level of involvement to an extreme and, in each situation, it led to my frustration.

Therein lies the challenge of leadership – finding the right balance. The quest for balance doesn't just relate to the level of involvement either; it permeates every aspect of managing people. Think about these other leadership dimensions:

- If a leader is too emotional, there is unnecessary drama in the office. If a leader is emotionless, the organization feels cold and callous.
- If a leader is too optimistic, the company is overly aggressive and misses targets. If a leader is too pessimistic, the organization never pushes to new levels of performance.
- If a leader is too aggressive, the organization might cut corners and take too many risks. If a leader is overcautious, the company may miss out on important opportunities for fear of failure.
- If a leader is too nice, poor performers are rarely disciplined. If the leader is too mean, a toxic environment can exist that affects overall morale.
- If a leader is too knowledgeable, the team depends on him or her for all the answers. If a leader has only a limited understanding of the business, there is a lack of respect and the possibility that people could take advantage of the situation.

Finding balance as a leader is critical but determining the right balance in every leadership situation is difficult. It requires self-awareness and a willingness to listen to constructive feedback. Leaders who are looking for balance need to have an empathic ear to listen to employees' concerns. Leaders need to be sensitive to areas where they may be acting in an extreme manner.

If you think back on the last several months, were there times you acted in an extreme manner? How did your employees react? What was the feedback? Consider any adjustments you need to make to become more balanced. Leaders who operate in the extremes for extended periods of time are less effective. Find the right balance that works with your team to get the best organizational outcomes.

The Paradox of Leadership

A leader is best when people barely know he exists, when his work is done, his aim fulfilled, they will say: we did it ourselves. – Lao Tzu

Chinese philosopher and writer, Lao Tzu, captured the essence of perfect leadership. Leadership is at its best when a team is so intrinsically motivated to complete a goal that they forget where the objective actually originated. In the end, employees feel they did it themselves and they didn't even need a leader.

This is the paradox of leadership. Leadership matters because it is absolutely critical for building, coordinating, and motivating a group of people to accomplish complex and difficult tasks. On the other hand, leadership doesn't matter. An experienced team, properly motivated, can achieve difficult objectives with very little leadership involvement.

General George Patton understood this when he said, "Don't tell people how to do things; tell them what to do and let them surprise you with their results." Under his leadership, the Third Army swept across France, crossed the Rhine, and charged straight into the heart of Germany. In 1945, his troops captured more than 10,000 square miles of enemy territory in one 10-day march. In the end, Patton and his Army achieved their vision of liberating Germany from the Nazis.

Like other great leaders, Patton seemed to understand his role. He knew he didn't need to micromanage his troops to get them to do extraordinary things. He cast the vision, set the goals, established the boundaries, motivated his team, and got out of the way.

The French writer, poet, and pioneering aviator, Antoine de Saint-Exupery, captured the importance of casting the vision when he said, "If you want to build a ship, don't drum up people to collect wood and don't assign them tasks and work, but rather teach them to long for the endless immensity of the sea."

Too often, leaders think they need to know everything, direct every activity, and be involved in every decision. When you do that, the vision becomes yours, not theirs. In the end, you are limiting the success of the team. They will only be as good as you are. You will never be surprised with their results.

Along with casting the vision, leaders need to establish boundaries and set priorities. People need to know what is expected of them. Great leaders establish the norms and rules of the organization. They set expectations so everyone understands what to do.

A great example of this is the first CEO I served under, Percy Barnevik. As CEO of the multi-national engineering company ABB, Barnevik's priority was to move fast. He embedded a culture of decisiveness at all levels of the organization. He didn't want a slow-moving, cumbersome, command-and-control organization. Instead, he kept his operating units small, he limited the decisions coming out of headquarters, and he preached the importance of decisiveness.

I was running one of those small operating units at the time and it was one of the best jobs I ever had. Barnevik was decisive and he expected the same from his leaders. The company culture at that time reflected his personality. We moved fast and we fixed it along the way.

Barnevik trusted us to make decisions. He had faith in his business unit leaders. He knew that we would occasionally make mistakes but he trusted us to always make it right. There was a culture of speed, decisiveness, and forgiveness. If you made a bad decision, it was not the end of your career. You were expected to fix it and move on.

The paradox of leadership is that it both matters and doesn't matter. It matters that leaders build a strong team with great employees. It matters that they cast a vision and set goals. They also need to establish boundaries and set priorities, making sure expectations are clear.

On the other hand, leadership doesn't matter. There comes a time when leaders need to simply get out of the way. Experienced teams, properly motivated, will achieve difficult objectives with very little leadership involvement. People will always surprise you with their results.

Lao Tzu may have captured the essence of perfect leadership – to create a team of people so intrinsically motivated to complete a goal that they forget where the objective actually came from. Maybe the most important role of leadership is how John Quincy Adams defined it: "If your actions inspire others to dream more, learn more, do more and become more, you are a leader."

CONCLUSION

A life is not important except in the impact it has on other lives. – Jackie Robinson

As I write this, I'm looking at a framed picture on the wall in my office of the 160 employees I led at my first manufacturing plant. Each person signed the matte surrounding the photograph, many leaving words of encouragement. This is one of my most prized possessions. I'd like to think I was a good leader and I made an impact on each of their lives but the truth is they impacted me so much more. Twenty years later, I can't remember all the financial success or awards we won but I can remember the laughter, the tears, the meals, the inside jokes, the employee meetings, and the holiday parties. I remember the long days counting physical inventory and the challenge of helping in the shipping department on the last day of the month. This picture is a reminder of what is really important – *people*.

Leadership is a people business and if we ever forget that, we become less effective in our roles as leaders. When you have the watch, you are responsible for your team. Your actions have a deep impact on their lives and careers.

Simon Sinek's best-selling leadership book, *Start with Why: How Great Leaders Inspire Everyone to Take Action*, focuses on only one element of leadership – social influence. In his view, influence should be at the top of the leadership triangle. He holds Steve Jobs up as a leader who mastered the ability to inspire millions. While I agree Jobs had a remarkable impact on the world, in all estimations, he was a total jerk. No one wanted to work for him.

Imagine if Steve Jobs had the power to influence *and* treated people with respect as well. Where would Apple be today if it hadn't been so dependent on the inspiration of one charismatic leader? Jobs never became the Lao Tzu version of a perfect leader. He wasn't the type of leader who would allow people to "barely know he existed." Jobs had to be the center of attention. He had to be the leader on the top of the leadership triangle and, as it seems to be playing out, his company was only as strong as his over-sized personality. Maybe Sinek should have written a book called, *Start with Who: How Great Leaders Put People First.* Leaders who focus on leading people well will be more effective in the long run. Their teams will continue to be successful long after the leader is gone because they have become intrinsically motivated and don't need the external motivation of a larger-than-life leader.

There is a leadership crisis in business today. Too many managers have moved into leadership positions who either lack the formal training or the desire to be a great leader. They are leaders in name only. These are the bosses who frustrate employees, cause dissatisfaction in the workplace, and create widespread apathy. The problem is significant and widespread, which is why more than 70% of employees are disengaged at work and half of the U.S. workforce is actively looking for another job. There are far too many bad bosses in business today but it doesn't have to be this way.

Leadership is difficult but not impossible. It's complex yet it's simple. To be a great leader, you don't have to read 15,000 books, but you do have to focus on how you interact with the people who work for you. At the end of the day, leadership is about people. As Kevin Kruse reminds us, leadership is about how you influence people to achieve a goal. By his definition and my experience, leadership comes down to just three elements – people, influence, and a goal. Great leaders learn to coordinate and balance these elements effectively.

If you're a leader, you have the watch and you're in charge. You are not only responsible for the results of the organization, but you are also responsible for your employees. In the Navy, watchstanders had to be vigilant. They were responsible for the safe operation of the ship and needed to be ready to respond to emergencies and other situations quickly. If you had the watch, you needed to be awake and alert because you literally had the lives of your shipmates in your hands.

As a watch officer on the *USS Tennessee*, I took my job seriously. As a leader of a business, I do the same. I know I'm responsible for my team and I understand my actions have a deep impact on their lives and careers. It's not easy and I don't do it for the paycheck, the prestige, or the power. I do it for my team because I have the watch.

Made in the USA
Columbia, SC
17 February 2020